ANIMAL ARTS AND CRAFTS

CREEPY-CRAWLY CRAFTS

Annalees Lim

Gareth Stevens
PUBLISHING

CONTENTS

SAFETY PRECAUTIONS

We recommend adult supervision at all times while doing the activities in this book. Always be aware that craft materials may contain allergens, so check the packaging for allergens if there is a risk of an allergic reaction. Anyone with a known allergy must avoid these.

- Wear an apron and cover surfaces.
- Tie back long hair.
- Ask an adult for help with cutting.
- Check materials for allergens.

BEFORE YOU BEGIN

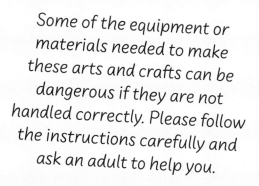

Are creepy-crawly animals your favorite? Would you like to make some of your own and find out lots of fun facts about them along the way? Follow the step-by-step instructions on each page to make bumblebees, dragonflies, spiders, and much more.

Some of the equipment or materials needed to make these arts and crafts can be dangerous if they are not handled correctly. Please follow the instructions carefully and ask an adult to help you.

A lot of the projects use paint and glue. Always cover surfaces with layers of old newspaper. Whenever you can, leave the project to dry before moving on to the next step. This avoids things getting stuck to each other or paint smudging.

So, do you have your craft supplies ready? Then get set to make your creepy-crawly arts and crafts and discover what makes each animal so special!

SPARKLY LADYBUG

Ladybugs have hard wing cases that protect their folded wings. This ladybug's wing cases are covered in glitter so they shimmer and sparkle!

YOU WILL NEED:

- Egg carton
- Glue
- Paintbrush
- Red glitter
- Black sequins
- Black card stock
- Scissors
- Pencil
- Ruler
- Compass
- Glue stick
- Googly eyes
- An adult to help you

Ask an adult to help you cut out a section of egg carton for the ladybug's body. It should be about 1.5 inches (4 cm) high.

Cover the body in glue and sprinkle red glitter all over it. Leave it to dry.

Ask an adult to help you use a compass and scissors to cut out a circle of black card stock that is bigger than the ladybug's body.

Cut out two thin strips of black card stock, 1.5 inches (4 cm) long. Stick these onto the black circle and curl the ends using your pencil.

Stick the body onto the black card stock circle using glue. Glue on black sequins and googly eyes to finish your ladybug.

DID YOU KNOW?

The bright color and spots on a ladybug's wing cases are a warning to birds: Don't eat this animal because it tastes bad!

LADYBUG FACTS!

Ladybugs are beetles, the largest group of insects. They eat aphids and other small insects.

The ladybug's life cycle goes like this: egg, larva, pupa, adult ladybug. This is a ladybug larva.

EWEL BEETLE FACTS!

Jewel beetles are insects called true bugs. A true bug uses its sharp mouthparts to pierce a plant and suck up its juices as liquid food. Yum!

JEWEL BUG

Jewel beetles are some of the most colorful insects in the world! Use this fun scratch method to make your own shimmering bug.

YOU WILL NEED:

- Two pieces of white card stock
- Green paper
- Blue, green, red, and black crayons
- Toothpick
- Scissors
- Green felt-tip pen
- Glue stick
- Thin black marker
- An adult to help you

1

Use the blue, green, and red crayons to make a pattern on the white card stock.

2

Cover your crayon markings with black crayon.

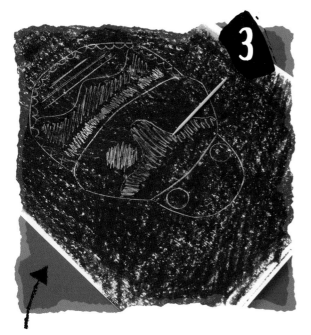

Use a toothpick to scratch off the black crayon layer to draw your jewel beetle. Cut it out.

Cut out leaf shapes from green paper. Use a green felt-tip pen to add leaf veins. Glue the leaves onto a piece of white card stock.

Glue your bug onto the leafy background. Add its legs and antennae with the black marker.

DID YOU KNOW?

Many jewel beetles are shiny and metallic. This is called iridescence.

CATERPILLAR COLLAGE

Caterpillars come in many different sizes and colors. Choose lots of colored, patterned paper to create your caterpillar collage!

YOU WILL NEED:

- Lots of colored, patterned paper
- Scissors
- Glue stick
- Two pieces of green card stock
- Pencil
- Black felt-tip pen
- Googly eyes
- Compass
- An adult to help you

Fold one sheet of green card stock in half, open it up, and fold each side into the center. Now you have three folds in the card stock. Number them 1–3, from left to right.

Fold the right-hand side so that it lines up with fold 1. Open it up again. Fold the left-hand side so that it lines up with fold 3 and open it up again.

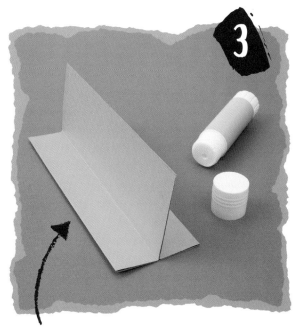

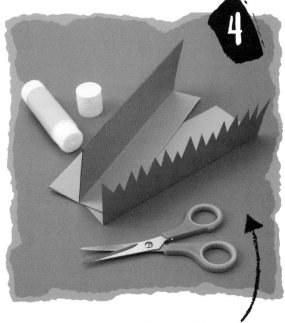

Fold the paper using the creases to create a T shape. Glue the folds into place.

Cut the short edge of the other sheet of green card stock to look like grass. Fold it and stick it to the T-shaped card stock.

Cut out circles from the colored paper. Stick them onto the green card stock to form the body of a caterpillar. Draw its legs in black felt-tip pen and stick on googly eyes. Add two strips of paper to make antennae!

DID YOU KNOW?

A caterpillar eats a lot! It sheds its skin so it can grow.

11

CATERPILLAR FACTS!

Like most insects, a caterpillar hatches from an egg. It is the young of a butterfly or moth. It grows and grows until it is time to change into an adult.

monarch butterfly egg

monarch caterpillar

12

BUTTERFLY FACTS!

Caterpillars eat plants, but butterflies and moths drink flower nectar. Look how this butterfly is using its long tongue like a drinking straw. Once it has finished, its tongue rolls up under its head.

tongue

monarch butterfly

BUTTERFLY PAPER CHAIN

Butterflies have four brightly colored wings. Create a chain of butterflies with colorful wings to decorate your room!

YOU WILL NEED:

- Colored paper strips, 1 inch (2.5 cm) wide
- Scissors
- Ruler
- Tape
- Ribbon
- Stapler
- An adult to help you

Cut three paper strips so that one is 8 Inches (20 cm) long, one is 6 inches (15 cm) long, and one is 4 inches (10 cm) long. Staple them all together at one end.

Bend the paper strips so that the ends all line up, without making a crease in the paper. Staple them together. Repeat steps 1 and 2 to make a second wing.

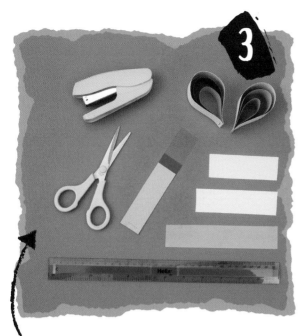

Cut three shorter strips, 6 inches (15 cm), 4.5 inches (11 cm), and 3.5 inches (9 cm) long. Join them by following steps 1 and 2. Make another one.

Use tape to join all four wings to make a paper butterfly.

Make as many paper butterflies as you want. Join them together to form a chain by stapling the top wings of each butterfly to each other. Tie a piece of ribbon to each end of the chain to hang it up.

DID YOU KNOW?

Butterflies use their wings to fly from plant to plant, sucking up nectar from flowers.

SNAIL STAMP

Most snails have a shell with a spiral shape. Create your own snails with this shell stamp!

YOU WILL NEED:

- 4 x 4 inch (10 x 10 cm) piece of cardboard
- Glue and string
- Paint and paintbrush
- Light blue card stock
- Green paper
- Colored paper
- White paper
- Felt-tip pen
- Scissors
- Glue stick
- Tape
- Googly eyes
- Tape measure
- An adult to help you

Cut three lengths of string, about 20 inches (50 cm) long. Use tape to join them together at one end. Braid the strings and use tape to attach their ends.

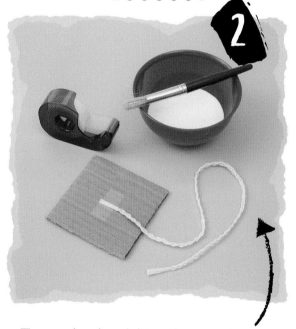

Tape the braid to the center of the cardboard square. Carefully cover the rest of the card with a layer of glue.

Glue the string onto the cardboard in a spiral shape. Keep the string as flat as possible. Leave it to dry.

Cut out a grass border from green paper and two snail body shapes. Glue all the pieces onto light blue card stock. Add googly eyes.

Cover the stamp with paint. Press it down on white paper to make a shell print. Lift it off and repeat. When they are dry, cut them out and stick them onto the snail bodies.

DID YOU KNOW?

Snails can seal themselves inside their shell and stay there for months! They do this if the weather is too hot and dry for them.

SNAIL FACTS!

Snails slide along on their slimy "foot." They belong to a large group of animals called mollusks.

A snail's eyes are on the ends of its two long tentacles. It can only really see the difference between light and dark.

PRAYING MANTIS FACTS!

There are over 2,400 different sorts of mantis, including the praying mantis. It lies in wait for an insect and then grabs it with its spiky front legs. Then it eats its prey alive!

A female praying mantis will often eat her mate, starting with his head!

PRAYING MANTIS

A praying mantis is hard to spot because it looks like the twigs and leaves it lives on. Make your own praying mantis to hide in plants around your home!

YOU WILL NEED:

- Plastic fork
- Green pipe cleaners
- Green electrical tape
- Green foam
- Green bendy straws
- Thin black marker
- Scissors
- Glue
- Ruler
- An adult to help you

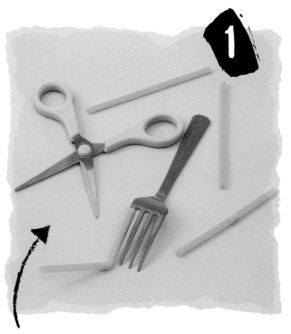

Cut off the bottom of the drinking straws so that they measure 3.5 inches (9 cm). Push them onto the outside prongs of the fork and bend them back.

Draw a face shape and eyes on green foam with a black marker. Cut out the face.

Tape the foam face onto the straws. Wind green electrical tape around the whole fork.

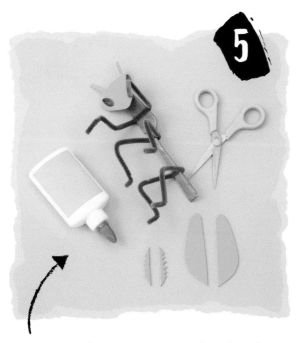

Make three pairs of legs by wrapping the center of each pipe cleaner around the top, middle, and bottom of the fork. Bend them into shape to make your praying mantis stand up.

Cut out foam shapes for the front legs and the back of the body. Glue them in place.

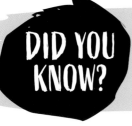

DID YOU KNOW?

This bug is called a praying mantis because it often folds its front legs into a praying position.

21

SHINY DRAGONFLY

Dragonflies are some of the fastest fliers in the insect world! Craft yours with wings that shimmer and glisten in the sunlight.

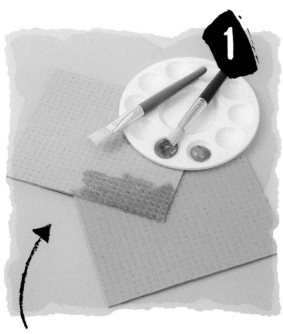

Paint two sponges with a layer of metallic paint. Remember to leave the sponges to dry before painting the other side.

Paint the wooden clothespin gold and leave it to dry.

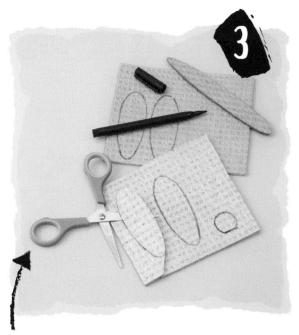

Cut out four oval shapes for the wings; a long, thin shape for the body; and a circle for the head. Cut out five small rectangles.

Use a marker to draw the veins of the wings onto each oval.

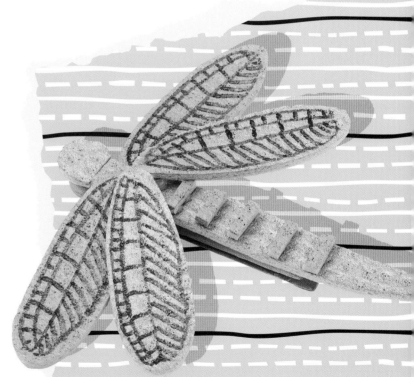

Glue the head and body onto the clothespin, and add the small rectangles. Glue on the wings and leave your dragonfly to dry.

DID YOU KNOW?

Dragonflies catch their food with their feet! They only eat prey that they have caught in flight.

DRAGONFLY FACTS!

A dragonfly can fly forward and backward, and it can hover. At rest, it holds its wings flat.

Dragonfly eyes are made up of thousands of tiny eyes. They have excellent eyesight. This helps them catch insects to eat.

BUMBLEBEE FACTS!

There are about 250 different kinds of bumblebees living around the world.

This bumblebee is drinking nectar. She uses her tongue to suck up the sweet liquid made inside the flower.

BUMBLEBEES

Bumblebees look a bit like honeybees, but they are bigger and hairier. Follow these steps to make fuzzy bumblebees using pipe cleaners.

YOU WILL NEED:

- Two black and two yellow pipe cleaners
- Thick plastic, such as an acetate sheet
- Scissors
- Googly eyes
- Fabric glue
- Pencil
- Ruler
- An adult to help you

Twist a black and a yellow pipe cleaner together at one end, so they are joined.

Start wrapping the pipe cleaners around your thumb. Finish by pulling your thumb out and pushing the ends of the pipe cleaners into the hole where your thumb was.

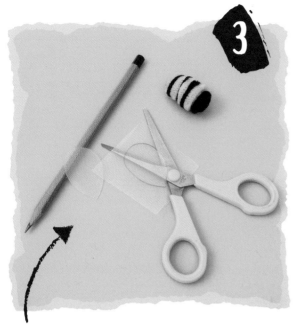

Draw two wing shapes on a plastic sheet and cut them out. Stick these wings to the body using fabric glue.

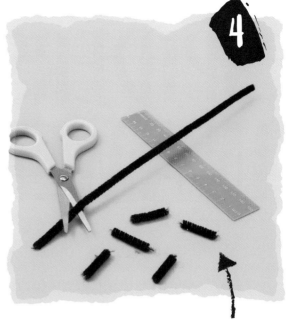

Cut six pieces of black pipe cleaner, 1 inch (2.5 cm) long. Bend them into leg shapes and glue them under the body.

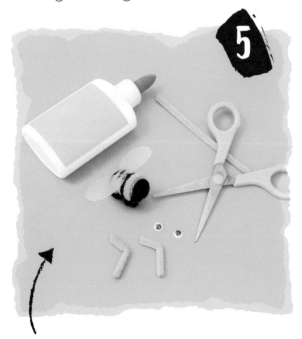

Cut two short pieces of yellow pipe cleaner and stick them into the head to make antennae. Glue some googly eyes onto the bumblebee's face.

DID YOU KNOW?

Most bumblebees only live about 28 days. Queens live longer.

SPIDERS IN A WEB

Spiders spin webs to catch food. Weave your very own sparkly spider's web and craft some googly-eyed spiders too!

YOU WILL NEED:

- Green and red tissue paper
- Silver embroidery thread
- Scissors
- Needle
- Purple card stock
- Glue
- Black pipe cleaners
- Googly eyes
- An adult to help you

Scrunch up two pieces of red tissue paper into a ball. Make a smaller ball with another piece of tissue paper. Glue both balls together to make the spider body and head.

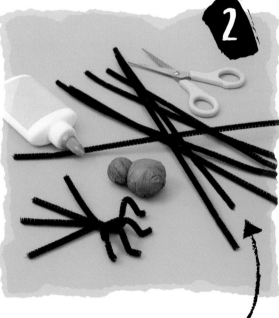

Cut two pipe cleaners in half and twist all four pieces together. Bend the ends of the pipe cleaners into leg shapes and glue them to the body.

Repeat steps 1 and 2 with green tissue paper. Stick googly eyes on each spider.

Starting in the center of the purple card stock, ask an adult to help you sew a star shape into the card stock using a double length of silver embroidery thread. Knot the end of the thread.

Ask an adult to help you use a second piece of thread to weave threads around your star shape to make a web. Place your spiders on the web!

DID YOU KNOW?

The silk that spiders make to weave their webs is finer than our hair, but it is stronger than steel!

TERMITE MOUND

YOU WILL NEED:

- Sand
- Paper plant pots (one small, one large)
- Glue
- Thin cardboard
- Pumpkin seeds
- Scissors
- Black and brown paint
- Paintbrushes
- An adult to help you

Some termites build homes, called mounds, which can be up to 30 feet (9 m) high! The model mound for your termites can be much smaller.

Ask an adult to help you cut thin cardboard into a wavy shape. Turn the large paper pot upside down and glue the small paper pot on top using glue.

Cover everything in a layer of glue and sprinkle sand over the top. Shake off any loose sand and leave to dry.

Mix the sand with glue and use the mixture to build turrets. Place them around the tall termite mound.

Cut some pumpkin seeds in half using scissors. Glue a whole pumpkin seed and half a seed onto the sand, to make the head and body of a termite. Make more termites.

Paint each termite brown. Then add legs using black paint.

DID YOU KNOW?

A lot of termites are born blind. They spend most of their lives inside the dark mound.

GLOSSARY

insect an animal with six legs and a body in three parts

larva insect young

life cycle the different stages of life for a living thing

mate the partner of an animal

mollusk an animal with a soft body and no backbone

nectar sweet liquid made by flowers

praying when people are speaking to a god

prey an animal that is eaten by other animals

pupa the stage of an insect's life cycle when it is changing into an adult

tentacles long, thin parts of an animal's body that may be used to feel, grasp, or hold things

INDEX

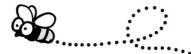

Please visit our website, www.garethstevens.com. For a free color catalog of all our high-quality books, call toll free 1-800-542-2595 or fax 1-877-542-2596.

Published in 2025 by
Gareth Stevens Publishing
2544 Clinton St.
Buffalo, NY 14224

First published in Great Britain in 2022 by Wayland

Copyright © Hodder and Stoughton, 2022 Wayland

Acknowledgements:
Shutterstock: Jolanda Aalbers 6t; Helen J Davies 24; jan j photography 12t; Breck P Kent 12b; Maconline99 13; Slavik Rostovski 25; Tatyana Sanina 19; Sophiecat 6b; Haramaini Syarif 7; Yul38885 18.

Every effort has been made to clear copyright. Should there be any inadvertent omission please apply to the publisher for rectification.

Cataloging-in-Publication Data
Names: Lim, Annalees.
Title: Creepy-crawly crafts / Annalees Lim.
Description: New York : Gareth Stevens Publishing, 2025. | Series: Animal arts and crafts | Includes glossary and index.
Identifiers: ISBN 9781538294413 (pbk.) | ISBN 9781538294420 (library bound) | ISBN 9781538294437 (ebook)
Subjects: LCSH: Handicraft--Juvenile literature. | Insects in art--Juvenile literature.
Classification: LCC TT160.L56 2025 | DDC 745.5--dc23

Editor, and author of the fact pages: Sarah Ridle
Design: Collaborate
Craft photography: Simon Pask, N1 Studios

CPSIA compliance information: Batch #CSGS25: For further information contact Gareth Stevens at 1-800-542-2595.

Find us on 🅵 📷